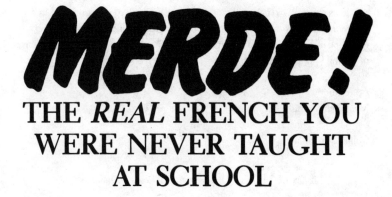

MERDE!

THE *REAL* FRENCH YOU WERE NEVER TAUGHT AT SCHOOL

GENEVIÈVE

Illustrated by MICHAEL HEATH

ATHENEUM   New York

Atheneum
Macmillan Publishing Company
866 Third Avenue, New York, N.Y. 10022
Collier Macmillan Canada, Inc.

Library of Congress Cataloging-in-Publication Data
Geneviève,
    Merde! : the real French you were never taught at
school.

    1. French language—Slang—Glossaries, vocabularies,
etc. 2. French language—Conversation and phrase
books—English. I. Title.
PC3741.G39   1986   447   85-47663
ISBN 0-689-11649-7

Macmillan books are available at special discounts for bulk purchases for sales
promotions, premiums, fund-raising, or educational use.
For details, contact:

    Special Sales Director
    Macmillan Publishing Company
    866 Third Avenue
    New York, N.Y. 10022

20 19 18 17 16 15 14 13 12 11

Printed in the United States of America

Designed by Cathryn S. Aison

A mes vieux (René et Nanette)
A mon frangin (Hervé)
A mon mec (Richard)
A mes gosses (Rupert, Oliver et Jamyn)

CONTENTS

PREFACE   ix
Guidance   ix

I. **THE MUSTS**   3
   Common Everyday Musts   3
   The Absolute Musts   15
      The MERDE Family   15
      The CHIER Family   19
      The CON Family   20
      The FICHER and FOUTRE Families   21

II. **VARIATIONS ON A THEME**   27
   Theme One: What an Idiot   27
   Theme Two: What a Pain   30
   Theme Three: I Don't Give a Damn   32

III. **THE BODY AND ITS FUNCTIONS**   35
   The Parts   35
   Bodily Functions   40
   Body Types   43

IV. THE WEIGHTY MATTERS
OF LOVE AND SEX
(National Obsession Number One)   49
The Protagonists   49
The Chase   55
Emotions and Conquest   57
Parties   61
Disasters   63

V. THE NO LESS WEIGHTY MATTERS
OF FOOD AND DRINK
(National Obsession Number Two)   67
Food   67
Drink   70

VI. HASSLING   74

VII. MONEY MATTERS   81

VIII. WORK AND SOCIAL STATUS   84
Work and Jobs   84
Social Status and Political Affiliation   87

IX. INDULGING IN RACISM, XENOPHOBIA
AND DISRESPECT FOR ONE'S ELDERS   91

X. TO EXIT RAPIDLY   94

XI. POSITIVE THINKING   96

XII. FOREIGN INVASIONS
OF THE LANGUAGE   98

XIII. YOUR FINAL EXAM   101

PREFACE

Do you remember when you were learning French at school and looked in vain through your dictionary for all the dirty words? Have you thought you had a reasonable command of the language, then seen a French film or gone to France only to find that you could barely understand a word? You were, of course, never taught *real* French by your boring teachers, who failed to give you the necessary tools of communication while stuffing the subjunctive imperfect down your throat. French *argot* (slang) is not just the dirty words (though, have no fear, you will find them here); it is an immensely rich language with its own words for very ordinary things, words that are in constant use. Here, then, is not an exhaustive or scholarly dictionary of *argot* (that would be ten times thicker) but a guide to survival in understanding everyday French as it is *really* spoken.

GUIDANCE

Asterisks after *argot* words indicate a degree of rudeness above the ordinary colloquial. Two asterisks show a whopper, although you should not assume that strength and rudeness cause a word to be used less frequently; *au contraire*.

When an English definition is underlined, that definition gives a good equivalent flavor, feeling and degree of rudeness of the French word. Good equivalents are not that common, so rely generally on the English definition for the meaning of the French word, on the asterisks for its strength and on the many examples for its usage. Just remember, to be authentic is to be rude.

I
THE MUSTS

COMMON EVERYDAY MUSTS

So many everyday words have their colloquial counterparts which appear constantly in conversation. The following is a list of the most frequently used and, therefore, most necessary ones, which do not fall into any of the neat categories of subsequent sections.

NECESSARY NOUNS

People

a fellow, a guy, a man	un type
	un gars
	un mec*
a woman	une bonne femme*
a chick, a broad	une gonzesse**

a kid	un/une môme
	un/une gosse
	un gamin, une gamine
what's-his-name	machin, machin-chouette
what's-her-name	machine, machine-chouette
a friend	un copain, une copine
Mrs., miss, ma, old lady	la mère (la mère Dupont a dit = old lady Dupont said)

MON SALOPARD DE FRANGIN S'EST FOUTU À LA FLOTTE ET SES GODASSES SONT FICHUES

HEATH

Mr., pop, old man	le père (le père Dupont = old man Dupont)
parents	les vieux
the old man (father)	le paternel le vieux
the old lady (mother)	la maternelle la vieille
a son	un fiston
son! young man! junior!	fiston!
a brother	un frangin
a sister	une frangine
a nasty person	un chameau (literally, a camel)
a bastard	un salaud** (ce salaud de Dupont = that bastard Dupont) un salopard**
a bitch	une salope** (cette salope de Marie = that bitch Marie)
a bastard or a bitch	une vache* (literally, a cow) une peau de vache* (literally, a cow's hide)
a shit	un fumier* (literally, manure)

| an asslicker | un lèche-cul** |
| a bootlicker | un lèche-bottes* |

Animals

a dog, a mutt	un cabot*
	un klebs*
	un klébard*
a bird	un piaf* (remember Edith Piaf?)

Things

nothing	quedale, or que dalle
a book	un bouquin
a car	une bagnole
a jalopy, a heap, a wreck	un tacot
a slow vehicle	un veau (literally, a calf)
a smoke, a butt	une sèche
water	la flotte
paper	du papelard
a rag (newspaper)	une feuille de chou (literally, a cabbage leaf)
	un canard
a bike	une bécane
	un vélo

a room	une piaule
the <u>sack</u> (bed)	le pieu le plumard (from "la plume" = the feather)
a lamp	une loupiote
the TV, the tube	la télé
a phone call	un coup de fil
a boat	un rafiot
a thing, a <u>thingumajig</u>	un bidule un truc un machin un fourbi un engin
the john, the <u>can</u>	les water (from "les WC" = the water closet) les chiottes**
a snag	un pépin
a mess, a shambles	la pagaille, la pagaïe
a foul-up, a mess	un bordel**

Clothes

clothes	les frusques (m.) les fringues (f.) les nippes (f.)
a hat	un bitos un galurin

a pair of pants	un falzar
a shirt	une liquette
a raincoat	un imper (short for "un imperméable")
shoes	les godasses (f.) les tatanes (f.)
outsize shoes, clodhoppers	les écrase-merde** (f.) (literally, shit squashers)
an umbrella	un pépin un pébroque
a ring	une bagouse
a suitcase	une valoche

NECESSARY ADJECTIVES

friendly and nice	sympa (short for "sympathique")
exhausting	crevant,e
incredibly funny	crevant,e tordant,e
funny	rigolo, rigolote
disgusting	dégueulasse* débectant,e* (from "débecter*" = to puke)
ugly, lousy	moche

8

useless, no good	à la gomme
	à la noix

NECESSARY VERBS

to understand	piger
not to understand a damn thing about	ne piger quedale à
to dig up, to find	dégoter, dégotter
to lose	paumer
to watch out for, to be careful about	faire gaffe à

to make a mistake	faire une gaffe (note the difference from the preceding expression) se gourer
to bust, to break	bousiller péter*
to have some nerve	avoir du culot être culotté,e avoir du toupet être gonflé,e (literally, to be swollen)
to go too far, to push	charrier
to be enthusiastic, to be crazy (about)	être un fana, une fana ("fana" is short for "fanatique"; c'est un fana de la voile = he's crazy about sailing)
to have a good time, to laugh	rigoler se marrer
to kid, to joke	rigoler (tu rigoles, non? = are you kidding?)
to grouse, to gripe	rouspéter (gives "un rouspéteur, une rouspéteuse" = a moaner, grumbler) râler (gives "un râleur, une râleuse" = a moaner, grumbler)

to be in a good mood	être de bon poil être bien vissé,e (literally, to be well screwed in) être bien luné,e
to be in a bad mood	être de mauvais poil être mal vissé,e être mal luné,e
not to make much of an effort	ne pas se fouler
to be lucky	avoir du bol avoir du pot
to be unlucky	manquer de bol manquer de pot
to rip off, to steal	chiper pincer piquer faucher barboter rafler
to lick someone's boots	faire de la lèche à quelqu'un*
to be pouring rain	flotter
to be stuck with	se farcir*

NECESSARY BITS AND PIECES

yes	ouais
OK	d'ac (short for "d'accord")

no way!	des clous! tintin!
so what?	et alors? ben quoi (ben = eh bien)
damn!	zut! la barbe!
goddammit! oh my God!	putain**! (literally, whore)
that damn...	ce putain de..., cette putaine de...**
you...	espèce de... (espèce de salaud = you bastard)
you... (pl.)	bande de... (bande d'idiots = you bunch of idiots)
extremely + an adjective	archi- (archi-dégueulasse = extremely disgusting
very, really	vachement drôlement rudement
shut up!	écrase*! ferme-la*! ta gueule**! ("gueule" is literally an animal's mouth, but is used pejoratively for people's mouths or faces)
I dare you!	chiche!

12

my ass!	mon cul**!
hi!	salut!
this afternoon	c't'aprèm (short for "cet après-midi)
what? huh?	hein?
phew!	ouf!
ow, ouch!	aie! ouille!
yuk!	beurk!

A FEW TIPS FOR CONSTRUCTING AUTHENTIC-SOUNDING SENTENCES

- Clip the end vowel off pronouns. Say "t'es sympa" instead of "tu es sympa."

- "Ce," "cet" and "cette" are clipped to become "c," "c't" and "c'te." Say "c'mec" (pronounced "smec") instead of "ce mec."

- Use "y'a" for "il y a" and "y'avait" for "il y avait."

- Omit the "ne" from the negative "ne ... pas." Say "j'sais pas" (pronounced "chais pas") instead of "je ne sais pas."

- Emphasize the subject by adding the relevant indirect pronoun at the end of the sentence. Say "j'sais pas, moi," "t'as du pot, toi." Or stress the subject by adding the noun that a subject pronoun connotes. Say "elles sont moches, ces godasses," "il est gonflé, c'mec."

13

NOW TRY YOUR HAND AT THE
FOLLOWING SENTENCES

1. C't'espèce de salaud frangin de Jojo m'a piqué ma bécane. Il a du toupet, c'mec.

2. "Passe-moi un coup de fil c't'aprèm." "D'ac."

3. Oh, putain, j'ai bousillé la bagnole du paternel.

4. Ton copain est vachement sympa, hein?

5. Aie! Fais gaffe, tu m'fais mal!

6. Il est pas rigolo, le gars. Il est toujours de mauvais poil.

7. J'pige quedale à c'bouquin, moi.

8. Allez, venez, les gars, à la flotte!

9. C'est moche; la mère machine-chouette a paumé son cabot.

10. Où est-ce que t'as dégotté c'truc dégueulasse?

11. Tu charries, ta piaule est un vrai bordel.

1. That Jojo's bastard of a brother has ripped off my bike. That guy has got some nerve.

2. "Give me a call this afternoon." "OK."

3. Oh, hell, I've totaled my old man's car.

4. Your friend is really nice, isn't he?

5. Ouch! Watch it, you're hurting me!

6. That guy isn't much fun. He's always in a bad mood.

7. I don't understand a damn thing about this book.

8. Hey, come on, fellows, let's jump in (that is, in the water)!

14

9. It's too bad; old lady what's-her-name has lost her dog.

10. Where did you find that disgusting thing?

11. It's too much, your room is a real mess.

THE ABSOLUTE MUSTS

THE MERDE** FAMILY

"Merde**" means literally and figuratively "shit." It is known in polite circles as "les cinq lettres" (we would say "a four-letter word"). But then, there are few such circles, and

the word is vital for communication with the natives. It does not have the impact and shock value of its English equivalent, so sprinkle liberally. The "merde**" family has several nominal, adjectival and verbal forms, so it can be, and is, handily inserted anywhere and anyhow.

NOUNS

la merde** = the <u>shit</u>
as in:

>J'ai marché dans de la merde**.
>I walked in some <u>dogshit</u>.

>Oh, merde** alors!
>Oh, shit! Oh, hell! Oh, damn!

and in the expressions:

>**être dans la merde****
><u>to be up shit's creek</u>

>**se foutre**** **dans la merde****
>to get it all wrong (literally, to put oneself in the shit)

>**ne pas se prendre pour de la petite merde****
>to take oneself very seriously, to think oneself great (literally, not to take oneself for small shit)

un emmerdement** = a real problem, trouble

>J'ai des emmerdements** avec ma bagnole.
>I'm having real trouble with my car.

un emmerdeur, une emmerdeuse** = a pain in the neck

>Ce type est un emmerdeur** de premier ordre.
>That fellow is a first-class pain in the neck.

16

le merdier** = a fine mess, a jam, a fix (literally, the shitpile)

> T''es dans un de ces merdiers**, toi alors!
> You sure are in a fine mess!

un petit merdeux, une petite merdeuse** = a little twerp

> Le môme du père Dupont est un vrai petit merdeux**
> Old man Dupont's kid is a real little twerp.

un démerdeur, une démerdeuse** = one who always manages, one who always gets what he/she wants (literally, one who always gets out of the shit)

> J'ai jamais vu une démerdeuse** comme Pascale.
> I've never known anyone always to get her own way like Pascale.

la démerde** = the art of being resourceful, of always landing on one's feet, of always getting what one wants (the French consider this, known also as "le système D," an art form)

Ce mec* est un champion de la démerde**.
This fellow is a master at landing on his feet.

des écrase-merde** (f.) = outsize/huge shoes (literally, shit-squashers)

Dis donc, t'as vu ses écrase-merde**?
Hey, have you seen his clodhoppers?

ADJECTIVES

emmerdant,e** = annoying, irritating, boring, a <u>pain in the neck</u>

Qu'est-ce qu'il est emmerdant** ton frangin!
What a pain your brother is!

emmerdé,e** = worried, annoyed

J'suis drôlement emmerdé**, j'ai paumé mon imper.
I'm really annoyed, I've lost my raincoat.

VERBS

emmerder** = to annoy, to irritate, to <u>give someone a pain in the neck</u>

Elle m'emmerde** cette bonne femme*, elle n'arrête pas de râler.
That woman gets on my nerves, she never stops complaining.

and in the expression:

Je l'emmerde**, je les emmerde****
To hell with him/her, to hell with them.

s'emmerder** = to be bored stiff

Qu'est-ce qu'on s'emmerde** ici.
It's a real bore here.

18

se démerder** = to manage, to get by

Ma copine se démerde** toujours pour avoir les meilleures places.
My girlfriend always manages to get the best seats.

THE CHIER** FAMILY

Anal matters again! Draw your own conclusions about their importance in the French language and psyche. "Chier**" means literally "to crap." The family of words derives from this meaning but has expanded to express intense annoyance and irritation. "Chiant**," for example, is one step further in rudeness than "emmerdant**," as "pain in the ass" is stronger than "pain in the neck."

VERBS

chier** = to <u>crap</u>

Son sale cabot a chié** partout dans ma piaule.
Her rotten old dog crapped all over my room.

faire chier** = to <u>give a real pain in the ass</u>

Ma maternelle me fait chier**.
My mother gives me a real pain in the ass.

envoyer chier quelqu'un** = to tell someone to fuck off

Un de ces jours, je vais envoyer mon vieux chier**.
One of these days I'm going to tell my old man to fuck off.

NOUNS

la chiasse** = the runs, and thence, fear

Rien que de penser aux examens, il a la chiasse**.
Just thinking about exams gives him the runs.

les chiottes** (f.) = the john, the can

> C'est par là, les chiottes**?
> Is the john that way?

une chierie** = a whole mess of problems; a drag

> Quelle chierie**, l'école!
> What a drag school is!

ADJECTIVE

chiant,e** = extremely irritating, boring, a <u>pain in the ass</u>

> Elle est chiante**, cette môme.
> That kid is a real pain in the ass.

> C'est chiant**, ça.
> That's a real drag.

THE CON** FAMILY

Physically, we haven't moved too far away, as we reach the third absolutely vital must. "Con**" means literally "cunt," but is used constantly and emphatically to indicate stupidity, thickness, somewhat as Americans use "asshole." As with "merde" and "chier," "con**" is everywhere in conversation and gives rise to a family of words.

NOUNS

un con, un connard**
une conne, une connasse, une connarde** = an idiot, a jerk, a fool

> Quel con**, ce mec*!
> What a damn fool that fellow is!

une connerie** = a stupidity, nonsense

> Ma frangine ne fait que des conneries**.
> My sister does nothing but stupid things.

> C'est de la vraie connerie**, ce bouquin.
> This book is nonsense.

ADJECTIVES

con, conne**
connard, connarde** = stupid, thick, dumb

> Les filles sont connes**.
> Girls are real idiots.

> Il a l'air con**.
> He looks stupid.

VERBS

déconner** = to fool around; to do foolish things; to bullshit

> Hé, les gosses, vous avez fini de déconner**?
> Hey, kids, have you finished fooling around?

> Ce machin déconne**.
> This thing is going nuts.

faire le con** = to act stupidly

> Faut toujours qu'il fasse le con**, ce mec*.
> That guy can never act sensibly.

THE FICHER* AND FOUTRE** FAMILIES

The verbs "ficher*" and "foutre**" are very useful and necessary: they can mean "to do," "to give," "to put," and they figure in many vivid expressions. "Foutre**" is the stronger of the two. Learn their usage through these examples; for the sake of easy reading, only "foutre**" will be used, but remember, either verb works.

21

VERBS

foutre** = to do

ne rien foutre** = not to do a damn thing

> Qu'est-ce que tu fous**?
> What the hell are you doing?

> Mon frangin ne fout** rien en classe.
> My brother doesn't do a damn thing in class.

foutre** une baffe = to give a slap

> Arrette ou je te fous** une baffe.
> Quit it or I'll slap you.

foutre** la paix à quelqu'un = to leave someone alone

> Foutez-nous** la paix!
> Leave us alone!

foutre** la trouille à quelqu'un = to scare the hell out of someone

> Ce klebs* a l'air enragé: il me fout** la trouille.
> This dog looks rabid; it scares the hell out of me.

foutre** = to put

> Où as-tu foutu** les clefs de la maison?
> Where the hell did you put the house keys?

foutre** le camp = to beat it, to get the hell out

> Allez, foutez-moi** le camp d'ici, bande de voyous.
> Go on, beat it, you punks.

> Hé, les gars, foutons** le camp avant que les flics n'arrivent.
> Hey, you guys, let's beat it before the cops come.

foutre** **au panier** = to throw into the wastepaper basket, to throw out

> Un de ces jours, j'vais foutre** la télé au panier.
> One of these days I'm going to throw the TV out.

foutre** **en l'air** = to throw out, to ruin

> La maternelle a foutu** toutes mes vieilles godasses en l'air.
> My mother threw out all my old shoes.

> Le mauvais temps a foutu** tous nos plans en l'air.
> The bad weather ruined all our plans.

foutre** à la porte = to kick out, to fire

> Ses vieux l'ont foutu** à la porte.
> His parents kicked him out of the house.
>
> Son patron l'a foutu** à la porte.
> His boss fired him.

se foutre** de quelqu'un = to make fun of someone, to take someone for a ride, to rip someone off

> Mes copains se sont foutus** de mon falzar.
> My friends made fun of my pants.
>
> Il s'est foutu** de toi le mec* qui t'a vendu cette bagnole.
> The fellow who sold you this car took you for a ride.

se foutre** de la gueule** des gens, se foutre** de la poire* du monde = to take everyone for a damn idiot

> Quoi, quinze francs pour un café? Vous vous foutez** de la gueule** des gens, non?
> What, fifteen francs for a cup of coffee? You've got to be kidding!

s'en foutre** de = not to give a damn about

> Je m'en fous** de ce que tu en penses.
> I don't give a damn what you think about it.

se foutre** dedans = to make a real mess (of something), to make a mistake

> Cette fois-ci, il s'est vraiment foutu** dedans.
> This time he really put his foot in it.
> (The French and the English expressions both imply stepping into something nasty.)

se foutre** parterre = to fall flat on one's face

> Fais gaffe, tu vas te foutre** parterre!
> Watch it, you're going to fall flat on your face!

The following two expressions are used only as given here:

Ça la fout** mal = It's a damned awkward situation.

Va te/Allez vous faire foutre**! = <u>Piss off! Fuck off! Stuff it!</u>

The participles "**fichu,e***" and "**foutu,e****" can also mean "done for," "finished," "ruined."

> La télé est foutue**.
> The TV has had it.

ADJECTIVES

The adjectival forms, "**fichu,e****" and "**foutu,e****," are used in the following expressions:

être mal foutu,e** = to feel rotten, ill; to work poorly, to be poorly laid out

> J'vais pas en classe aujourd'hui, j'suis mal foutu**.
> I'm not going to school today, I feel lousy.

> Ce magasin est mal foutu**.
> This shop is poorly laid out.

être bien foutu,e** = to have a great body; to work well, to be well laid out

> Elle est vachement bien foutue**, ta frangine.
> Your sister sure has a great body.

> Cette bagnole est drôlement bien foutue**.
> This car is really nifty.

être foutu,e** de faire quelque chose = to be liable to do something

> Fais gaffe, il est foutu** de tout bousiller.
> Watch it, he's liable to bust everything.

25

ne même pas être foutu,e** **de faire quelque chose** = not
even to be capable of doing something, not even to be willing
to do something

> Il n'est même pas foutu** de lui envoyer une carte pour
> son anniversaire.
> He can't even be bothered to send her a card for her
> birthday.

"Fichu,e*" and **"foutu,e**"** are used as "damned" etc.

> Ce foutu** temps est déprimant.
> This damned weather is depressing.

NOUNS

Two nouns belong to the foutre** family only:

le foutoir** = a shambles, a mess

> Ta piaule est un vrai foutoir**.
> Your room is a real mess.

la foutaise** = garbage

> C'est de la foutaise**, ton truc.
> That thing of yours is garbage.

II
VARIATIONS ON A THEME

Fact: the French individual feels superior to his fellow-man, foreign or not. Consequence: the French have a very wide selection of words to express their contempt for the intellectual, mental or spiritual inferiority of others as well as their annoyance derived from this contempt. The two following sections give you the range of words to which you might be subjected. The third offers a few replies.

THEME ONE: WHAT AN IDIOT

a jerk, an idiot, a fool

un con, une conne**, un connard, une connarde** une connasse** (remember Chapter I?) un couillon** (from "les couilles**" (f.) = testicles)

crazy, cracked, bonkers, nuts	dingue
	dingo
	cinglé,e
	zinzin
	timbré,e
	sonné,e
	siphonné,e
	tapé,e
	piqué,e
	toqué,e
	maboul,e
	loufoque
	marteau
	malade

All these and the following adjectives except "marteau" can be used as nouns when preceded by an article. For example,

C'est un vrai cinglé, ce type.
That fellow is a real nutcase.

Où as-tu dégotté une dingue pareille?
Where did you pick up such a crazy woman?

half-witted, mentally defective, retarded	débile
	demeuré,e
	arriéré,e
	crétin,e

a half-wit, a mental defective, a retard	un débile mental, une débile mentale
	un minus

degenerate	dégénéré,e
	taré,e

dim	paumé,e (remember "paumer" = to lose)

a clod, a twit, a fool	une andouille
	un corniaud
	une cruche
	une gourde
	un pied
	une patate
a nitwit	un ballot
silly	bébête
	cucul* (cucul la
	praline* = silly
	billy)
a silly goose	une bécasse
thick, dumb	con, conne**
	bouché,e
gaga, senile	gaga
	gâteux, gâteuse
weird	tordu,e
a scatterbrain	une tête de linotte
to go off one's rocker, to go around the bend, to flip out	dérailler (literally, to go off the rails) débloquer ne pas tourner rond
to have a screw loose	avoir une case de vide (literally, to have an empty compartment) être tombé,e sur le crâne (literally, to have fallen on one's skull)

to be as thick as a post	être con comme un balai**
	être con comme la lune* (this particular "lune" being not the moon, but the backside)
are you crazy?	ça va pas, non?

To lessen the offensiveness of a term, you can use "un peu...sur les bords." For example,

Elle est un peu zinzin sur les bords.
She's a bit on the cracked side (literally, she's a bit cracked around the edges).

THEME TWO: WHAT A PAIN

He/she is a real pain	Il/elle est casse-pieds
	Il/elle est emmerdant,e**
	Il/elle est chiant,e**
irritating	enquiquinant,e
	empoisonnant,e
boring	barbant,e
	rasant,e
	rasoir
to bore	barber
	raser (literally, to shave, and the shaving imagery to indicate boredom gives rise to an important gesture that you should be able to interpret, if you

	see a Frenchman raise his arm and stroke his cheek with the back of his fingers, you will know that he is indicating his boredom and irritation with a person or a situation)
deadly boring	assommant,e (assommer = to knock out)
to get on someone's nerves	taper quelqu'un sur les nerfs casser les pieds de quelqu'un les casser à quelqu'un (the "les" can refer to "pieds" or "couilles**")
to give someone a pain in the neck, ass; to piss someone off	faire suer quelqu'un (suer = perspire) faire chier quelqu'un** emmerder quelqu'un**
to irritate	enquiquiner empoisonner
to be fed up with	en avoir marre de en avoir plein le dos de en avoir ras le bol de en avoir plein le cul de**
what a drag!	quelle barbe!
not to be able to stand someone	ne pas pouvoir sentir quelqu'un ne pas pouvoir piffer quelqu'un*

	ne pas pouvoir blairer quelqu'un* ("le pif*" and "le blair*" mean the nose. These three expressions therefore literally mean "not to be able to smell someone," reminding us of the prominence of French noses)
not to be able to stand someone	ne pas pouvoir voir quelqu'un ne pas pouvoir voir quelqu'un en peinture ne pas pouvoir encaisser quelqu'un
to disgust	débecter*

THEME THREE: I DON'T GIVE A DAMN

<u>I don't give a damn</u>	je m'en fiche* je m'en fous** je m'en contrefiche* je m'en contrefous** je m'en balance* je m'en bats l'oeil*
<u>I don't give a fuck</u>	je m'en branle** (branler** = to masturbate; this expression is rather strong!)

   To say you don't give a damn about a certain thing, use any of the above followed by "de" and the object of your indifference. For example,

Je m'en fous de ton programme de télé, finis tes devoirs d'abord.
I don't give a damn about your TV program, finish your homework first.

REVIEW

Just a few sentences to see if you have absorbed the previous vocabulary.

1. Une gonzesse plutôt conne sortait avec un mec vachement sympa. Mais le type commençait à en avoir marre d'elle parce qu'elle pigeait jamais rien. Un jour, il en avait vraiment ras le bol. Il lui a dit de foutre le camp. "T'as du toupet," dit-elle, en lui foutant une baffe. La garce a appelé son cabot, en plus, pour déchirer le falzar du gars, ce qui l'a vraiment fait chier. "Salope!" cria-t-il, "Va te faire foutre!"

2. Je peux pas blairer ce débile de Jojo. Il emmerde le monde avec tous ses problèmes.

3. Les anglais sont complètement dingues, ils conduisent leurs bagnoles du mauvais côté.

4. C'est toujours les plus cons qui se prennent pas pour de la petite merde.

1. A pretty stupid woman was going out with a really nice guy. But the fellow was beginning to get fed up with her because she never understood anything. One day he'd really had it. He told her to beat it. "You've got some nerve," she said, slapping him. What's more, the cow called her dog to tear the guy's pants, which really pissed him off. "You bitch!" he yelled. "Fuck off!"

2. I can't stand that half-wit Jojo. He bugs everyone with all his problems.

3. The English are really crazy, they drive their cars on the wrong side.

4. It's always the dumbest who think they're so great.

Now, if you have mastered the previous chapters, we can begin to have fun, what with the body and sex coming up.

III
THE BODY AND
ITS FUNCTIONS

THE PARTS

the body

la carcasse (mainly in the expression "bouge ta carcasse" = budge, move!)

the head

le caillou (particularly in the expression "pas un poil sur le caillou" = as bald as a billiard ball, literally, not a hair on the stone)
le crâne (literally, the skull)

the nut

la citrouille (literally, the pumpkin)

the brain, the head

le ciboulot

the brain	les méninges (mainly in the expression "se creuser les méninges" = to rack one's brain)
the face, the <u>mug</u>	la gueule** la tronche* la bouille la trogne*
hair	les tifs (m.)
the schnoz, the nose	le pif* le blair*
the eyes	les mirettes (f.)
the ears	les esgourdes (f.)
the mouth	le bec* (literally, the beak) la gueule**
the lips	les babines (f.)
the mustache	les bacchantes (f.)
the beard	la barbouze
the hand	la paluche* la pince (serrer la pince = to shake hands) la patte* (bas les pattes* = hands off)
the biceps (muscles)	les biscoteaux (m.)
the leg	la patte* la guibole*

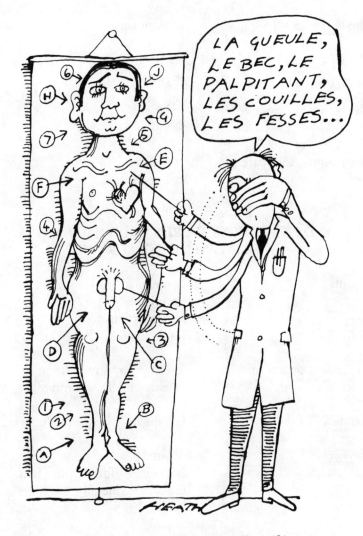

the legs	les quilles* (f.)
the thighs (heavy female ones)	les jambons* (m.; literally, the hams) les gigots* (m.; literally, the legs of lamb)
the foot	le panard*

the ticker (heart)	le palpitant
the guts	les boyaux* (m.) les tripes* (f.)
the belly	le bide* le bidon*
the paunch, the spare tire	la bedaine la brioche

AND NOW THOSE WORDS YOU'VE BEEN LOOKING ALL OVER FOR

the tits	le nichons* (m.) les miches* (f.) les tétons* (m.) les doudounes* (f.)
the genital organ, male or female	le zizi (a word used from early childhood onward)
the dick	la kiquette*, la quéquette*
the cock	la bitte** la queue** (literally, the tail) la verge** (literally, the rod) le zob** la pine**
the balls	les couilles** (f.)
the family jewels	les bijoux de famille
the pussy	le chat* la chatte* le con**

38

LE BEAU CHAT

the clit

the bottom, the buns, the backside

la praline* ("praline" is a sugared almond and the use of the word for clit comes from the similarity in shape)

l'arrière-train
les fesses* (f.; a useful expression to describe others, not yourself, is

	"avoir le feu aux fesses*" = to be in a hurry)
	le derche
the ass	la lune*
	le cul** ("le papier-cul**" or "pécu**" from the initial "p" for "papier" + "cul**" = toilet paper)
the rump	la croupe*
the asshole	le trou de balle**

BODILY FUNCTIONS

to cry	chialer*
to be tired	être crevé,e
	être vanné,e
to be washed out	être lessivé,e (la lessive = the washing)
to sleep	roupiller
	pioncer
to take a catnap	pousser un roupillon
to be dying of cold, heat, hunger, thirst	crever de froid, de chaud, de faim, de soif
to be cold	cailler (as in "je caille" = I'm freezing)

to catch a cold	attraper la crève
to be ill	avoir la crève
to puke	dégobiller* dégueuler**
to grow old, to be getting on	prendre de la bouteille prendre du bouchon
to kick the bucket, to croak, to die	crever* (note the versatility of the word, which literally means "to burst," and make sure you learn the variations of use above as they do make for variations of meaning) caner* claquer* clamecer* casser sa pipe
a stiff (corpse)	un macchabée, un macab*
to stink (applied only to living creatures)	puer le bouc (literally, to smell of goat) puer le fauve (literally, to smell of wild animal)
to stink (generally applicable)	puer cocoter* fouetter* schlinguer*
to burp	roter
to piss	pisser* faire pipi (the childish term)

41

to <u>crap</u>	chier** faire caca (the childish term)
to <u>wipe one's ass</u>	se torcher le cul**
<u>shit</u>	la merde**
<u>turds</u>	les étrons (m.)
to <u>fart</u>	péter* (this verb gives rise to a few useful expressions:

péter plus haut que son
cul** = to think too
highly of oneself; literally,
to fart higher than one's
ass
péter le feu* = to be full
of energy; literally, to fart
fire
un pète-sec* = a strict
disciplinarian; literally, a
clean, dry farter

a <u>fart</u>	un pet*
to <u>have a hard-on</u>	bander** avoir la tringle**
to <u>jerk off</u>, to masturbate	se branler** se tripoter*

BODY TYPES

to be striking	avoir de la gueule
a handsome young thing (male)	un beau gosse
to be well endowed (both sexes)	être bien monté,e
naked	à poil
a string bean (both sexes)	une grande asperge une grande bringue une grande perche

43

a puny runt	un avorton** (literally, the leftover from an abortion) un résidu de fausse couche** (literally, the leftover from a miscarriage)
a midget	un nabot
a skinny bones	un maigrichon, une maigrichonne
as thin as a rake	maigre comme un clou
a great hulking brute	une armoire à glace (literally, a wardrobe) un balaise un malabar
big, large	mastoc maousse
brawny, well built	baraqué,e
a big, tough guy	un casseur (literally, one who breaks things)
a large woman, a horse	un grand cheval une jument (literally, a mare)
a dumpy little woman	un pot à tabac (literally, a tobacco pot)
a really ugly, stubby woman, a dog	un boudin* (literally, black pudding, a stubby sausage)
mannish (said of a woman)	hommasse

a big fatso	un gros patapouf un gros plein de soupe
a fat slob	un gros lard
to have big tits	avoir du monde au balcon

to be curvaceous	être bien roulée
	être bien balancée
	être bien carrossée (la
	    carrosserie = the car
	    body)

a handsome morsel	un beau morceau

to be flat-chested	être plate comme une
	    limande (la limande =
	    the sole)
	être plate comme une
	    planche à pain (literally,
	    to be as flat as a bread
	    board)

to be bald	ne pas avoir un poil sur le caillou
to be going bald	perdre ses plumes se déplumer
a wig	une moumoute
to be hard-of-hearing	être dur,e de la feuille
deaf	sourdingue
to have cauliflower ears	avoir les oreilles en feuille de chou

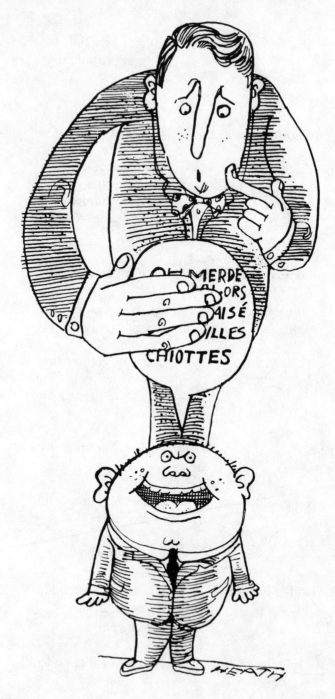

to be cross-eyed	avoir un oeil qui dit merde à l'autre**
near-sighted	bigleux, bigleuse
dirty	cracra, crado, cradingue, cradoc (all derived from "crasse" = filth)
to have dirty fingernails	avoir les ongles en deuil (literally, to have one's nails in mourning)

IT'S TIME TO PRACTICE YOUR EXPERTISE

1. Les zizis de vieille bonne femme, ça pue le fauve.

2. Les français ont des pifs énormes.

3. Un beau gosse ne sortirait jamais avec un boudin comme elle.

4. Hé, merde, ça schlingue ici. Y'a un salaud qui a pété! C'est dégueulasse, je vais dégobiller.

5. Ce mec a une gueule qui ne me revient pas.

6. Une gonzesse bien foutue a de longues guiboles, de beaux nichons, un petit cul mignon et un chat parfumé.

7. T'as vu cette espèce d'avorton culotté qui se branle chaque fois qu'il voit la belle Marie?

8. Son paternel a la crève, on dirait qu'il va claquer.

9. Je suis crevé, je vais juste pousser un roupillon.

10. Tes tifs sont drôlement cracra.

1. Old ladies' cunts stink.

2. The French have huge noses.

3. A handsome young thing would never go out with a dog like her.

4. Hey, shit, it stinks here! Some bastard's farted! It's disgusting, I'm going to puke.

5. That fellow's got a mug that I really don't like.

6. A well-built chick has long legs, pretty tits, a cute little ass and a sweet-smelling pussy.

7. Have you seen that cocky runt who jerks off whenever he sees lovely Marie?

8. His old man is ill, it looks as if he'll croak.

9. I'm dead tired, I'll just take a snooze.

10. Your hair is really dirty.

IV
THE WEIGHTY MATTERS OF LOVE AND SEX
(National Obsession Number One)

THE PROTAGONISTS

WOMEN

a girl, a chick

une nana
une nénette
une gonzesse**
une souris*

his girlfriend

sa pépée*
sa petite amie

his loved one (ironical)

sa dulcinée

his woman, his <u>broad</u>

sa julie*
sa poule**

his old lady (wife)

sa bergère*
sa bobonne

an innocent, naïve young thing	une oie blanche
a virgin	une pucelle
a spinster	une vieille fille
a coy hypocrite	une sainte nitouche
a shrew	une mégère
a bitch	une garce* une salope**
a stuck-up female	une pimbêche
a cock-teaser	une allumeuse* (from "allumer" = to inflame, to set on fire)
a seductress	une vamp
sexy	sexy
an easy lay	un paillasson* (literally, a doormat)
to be an easy lay	avoir les cuisses légères* (literally, to have light thighs)
a man-eater	une mangeuse d'hommes
a kept woman, a mistress	une femme soutenue
a slut, a tramp	une pouffiasse** une roulure**

a whore, a hooker	une pute*
	une putain*
	une morue**
a lady of the night	une fille de joie
a prostitute who solicits from cars	une amazone*
to solicit	racoler
to walk the streets	faire le trottoir
	faire le tapin*
	faire de la retape*
a whorehouse	un bordel
	une maison close
	une maison de passe
	un claque*
the madam	la maquerelle*
a dyke	une gouine**

MEN

a fellow, a guy	un type
	un gars
	un mec*
her boyfriend	son petit ami
	son jules*
a suitor	un soupirant
a virgin	un puceau
a confirmed bachelor	un vieux garçon

a stay-at-home	un pantouflard (from "la pantoufle" = the slipper)
a male chauvinist pig	un phallocrate (from "le phallus") un phallo
a smooth talker	un baratineur
a womanizer	un coureur un cavaleur
one who likes to go on the prowl for a pickup (but not involving prostitution)	un dragueur
a playboy	un tombeur*
to be a sex maniac	avoir le sang chaud (literally, to be hot-blooded)
a sex maniac	un chaud-lapin* (literally, a hot rabbit) un tringlomane** (from "tringler**" = to screw)
an exhibitionist, a lecher	un satyre
to suffer from middle-aged horniness	avoir le démon de midi*
to be a groper, a feeler	avoir la main baladeuse (literally, to have a wandering hand)
a cuckold	un cocu*
a gigolo	un gigolo

a pimp	un maquereau*
	un hareng* (notice the fishy teminology around prostitution, "le maquereau" being literally a mackerel, "le hareng" a herring and in the female section, "la maquerelle" a female mackerel, "la morue" a cod)
	un souteneur
a fag, a queer	un pédé*, une pédale* (from "le pédéraste")
	une tante*, une tantouse* (literally, an auntie)
	une tapette*
	une lope*
	une grande folle*, une folle*
a transvestite	un travelot*, un trav*

GENERAL DESCRIPTIVE TERMINOLOGY

sexy	sexy
sex appeal	le sex-appeal
to be trendy	être dans le vent (literally, to be in the wind, that is, to fly with the wind)
a trendy young thing	un minet, une minette
to be striking and elegant	avoir du chien
	avoir de la gueule

53

to be popular with the opposite sex	avoir du succès auprès du sexe opposé
easygoing	relaxe
a stay-at-home	un pot-au-feu ("le pot-au-feu" is a boiled beef and vegetable dish)
a show-off	un m'as-tu-vu
full of oneself	puant,e (remember "puer" = to stink)
snobbish, stuck-up	snob bêcheur, bêcheuse
fickle	volage
a reveler, a fast liver	un noceur, une noceuse
base, vile	immonde
corrupt	pourri,e (pourri = rotten)
twisted	tordu,e
dirty-minded	cochon, cochonne grossier, grossière
depraved	vicelard,e
obsessed	obsédé,e
repressed	refoulé,e frustré,e
masochistic	maso

to be obsessed with sex	être porté,e sur la chose
to be a cradle-robber	les prendre au berceau
to be AC-DC	marcher à la voile et à la vapeur (literally, to function by sail and steam)

THE CHASE

to go on the prowl, to pick up	draguer
to look for a piece of ass	chercher un peu de fesse*
to give someone the eye	faire de l'oeil à quelqu'un
to make sheep eyes at someone	faire les yeux doux à quelqu'un
to devour someone with one's eyes	manger quelqu'un des yeux
to ogle	lorgner zieuter (from "les yeux," pronounced "les zieu")
to cast lustful looks on	reluquer*
to hang around, to come sniffing around	rôder autour
to sweet-talk	baratiner faire du baratin à faire du plat à faire du gringue à

smooth talk, sweet talk	le baratin
to be taken in by someone's smooth talking	se laisser prendre au baratin de quelqu'un
to be attracted by	taper dans l'oeil de quelqu'un
to make a hit	faire une touche
to flirt	flirter
flirting	le flirt
love at first sight	le coup-de-foudre (literally, the bolt of lightning)
the rendezvous	le rencard
to play footsy with	faire du pied à faire du genou à
to flatter and fondle	faire des mamours à
to feel up	faire des papouilles à
to pet	peloter*
petting	le pelotage*
to paw	tripoter*
to leap on	sauter sur
to neck	se bécoter

56

a kiss	une bise
	un bisou
	un bécot
come up and see my etchings	venez voir mes estampes japonaises
my darling	mon chéri, ma chérie
	mon chou
	mon petit chou
	mon cocot, ma cocotte
my darling (woman only)	ma biche (literally, my doe)

EMOTIONS AND CONQUEST

to hit it off	avoir les atomes crochus (literally, to have hooked atoms)
to have a crush on	avoir le béguin pour
to have a soft spot for	avoir un faible pour
to be besotted by	s'enamouracher de
to be smitten by someone	être mordu,e de quelqu'un avoir quelqu'un dans la peau (literally, to have someone under one's skin)
to be mad about	être fou, folle de aimer à la folie
to live on love alone	vivre d'amour et d'eau fraîche

to find the man/woman in a million	trouver la perle (literally, to find the pearl) trouver l'oiseau rare (literally, to find the rare bird)
to get one's clutches into	mettre le grapin sur*
to strip	se foutre à poil**
to have it off, to make love with	s'envoyer* se farcir* se payer* se taper*
to screw, to lay a woman	culbuter une femme* tomber une femme* sauter une femme*
to fuck	baiser** (beware! "le baiser" = the kiss, "embrasser" = to kiss. So never say "je l'ai baisée" when you only mean "I kissed her" because what you are then saying is "I fucked her," a completely different kettle of fish) tringler**
the bedroom	le baisodrome** (derived from the above)
to get laid	se faire sauter*
to dip one's wick, to get it wet	tremper son biscuit*

a one-night stand	un amour de rencontre
a condom, a rubber	une capote anglaise (Just let that sink in. It gives you food for thought about the historical antagonism. You might be interested to know that the English call a rubber a "French letter" . . . sweet revenge)
feats, sexual exploits	les exploits (m.)
to make love in a slow, conventional, unexciting way	faire l'amour à la papa
to deflower	dépuceler passer à la casserole** (also means "to rape")
to come	jouir** prendre son pied**
climax	l'extase (f.)
to give a blow job	faire le pompier** faire une pipe**
69	le soixante-neuf**
to butt-fuck	enculer** emmancher** enfoirer**
to make love doggy-style	baiser en levrette** (literally, to fuck like a greyhound bitch)

60

a sleepless night	une nuit blanche

PARTIES

to get all dolled/dressed up	se nipper
	se saper
a party (with dancing)	une surprise-party
	une surboum
	une boum
to whoop it up	faire la bringue
	faire la bombe
	faire la noce
	faire la foire
	faire la bamboula
	faire la nouba
to carouse	faire ribote
to get an eyeful	se rincer l'oeil
dirty jokes	les histoires paillardes
	les histoires salées
obscenities	les ordures (f.)
	les saletés (f.)
	les horreurs (f.)
a wife-swapping party with two couples	une partie carrée*
an orgy	une partouse*
to participate in an orgy	partouser*
one who likes orgies	un partouzard*

a sexual orgy involving young girls below the age of consent	un ballet rose
a sexual orgy involving young boys below the age of consent	un ballet bleu
dirty movies, porno flicks	les films porno
porno press	la presse du cul**
a dirty newspaper	un journal de fesse*
a drug addict, a junkie	un toxico
marijuana, weed, grass, dope	la marie-jeanne
LSD	l'acid
an LSD trip	un trip
a narcotic drug	un stup (short for "le stupéfiant" = the narcotic drug)
heroin, smack	la chnouffe*, la schnouff*
to get a fix	se fixer* se schnouffer* se shooter*

DISASTERS

to be hanging around waiting, to be <u>cooling one's heels</u>	faire le poireau (le poireau = the leek) poireauter
to stand someone up	poser un lapin à quelqu'un
gossip	les ragots (m.)
to gossip	jacter
to <u>lead on</u>	faire marcher
to break hearts	faire des ravages (le ravage = devastation)
to dump, to <u>jilt</u>	plaquer laisser tomber laisser choir
to <u>be down in the dumps</u>, to feel low and depressed	avoir le cafard
melodrama	le mélo
to <u>take someone for a ride</u>	avoir quelqu'un (used most often by the victim in the "passé composé," as in "il m'a eue" = he took me for a ride)
to <u>be had</u>	se faire avoir
to come home without having scored	revenir la bitte sous le bras** (remember "la bitte" = the cock?)

63

to steal someone's girlfriend	souffler la petite amie de quelqu'un barboter la petite amie de quelqu'un piquer la petite amie de quelqu'un pincer la petite amie de quelqu'un faucher la petite amie de quelqu'un
to be unfaithful, to cheat	faire des infidélités
to cuckold	cocufier* (note that "une veine de cocu" = the luck of the devil. It shows that, for the French, being unlucky in love gives you a good chance in other endeavors, so all is not lost and maybe face is saved)
to knock up, to impregnate	encloquer** mettre en cloque** (la cloque = the blister)
to be knocked up, to be pregnant	avoir le ballon*
a back street abortionist	une faiseuse d'ange**
to tie the knot	se mettre la corde au cou
the mother-in-law	la belle-doche*
a flock of kids	une ribambelle de gosses

the <u>clap</u>, V.D.
        la vérole
        la chtouille**
        la chaude-pisse** (literally,
          hot-piss)
        la chaude-lance**

NOW GET ON WITH IT

1. Les anglais sont tous des pédés; les français sont des chaud-lapins; les italiens sont des baratineurs.

2. Au fond, les mecs sont tous phallos.

3. Ta copine est une vraie pouffiasse, elle se fait sauter par tout le monde.

4. Fais gaffe au père Dupont: il a le démon de midi, il court après toutes les nanas du bureau, a la main baladeuse et te sautera dessus si tu te trouves seule avec lui.

5. Il est dingue de se mettre la corde au cou: il va se farcir une salope de belle-doche. M'enfin, peut-être qu'il a foutu sa dulcinée en cloque.

6. Y'a que les minables, les refoulés, les pourris et les pauvres cons qui partousent ou se shootent.

7. Quelle bêcheuse, ta frangine, avec tous ses petits minets!

8. Il a le cafard parce que sa nana l'a plaqué après deux ans.

9. Dis, t'as fais une touche avec le type là-bas, il n'arrête pas de te zieuter.

    I shouldn't have to give you the translation if you've been studying your vocabulary with diligence. But, anyway, I'll be generous.

1. Englishmen are all fags; Frenchmen are sex maniacs; Italians are smooth talkers.

2. Basically men are all chauvinist pigs.

3. Your friend is a real slut, she gets laid by everyone.

4. Watch old man Dupont: he's suffering from middle-age horniness, he chases all the girls in the office, he's a groper and he'll jump you if you're alone with him.

5. He's crazy to tie the knot; he's going to get stuck with a bitch of a mother-in-law. Well, maybe he's got his loved one "in trouble."

6. Only the pathetic, the repressed, the rotten and the poor jerks go to orgies or do drugs.

7. What a snob your sister is with her trendy friends!

8. He's depressed because his girlfriend dumped him after two years.

9. Hey, you've made a hit with that guy over there, he keeps on ogling you.

V
THE NO LESS WEIGHTY MATTERS
OF FOOD AND DRINK
(National Obsession Number Two)

FOOD

food, grub	la bouffe* la boustif* la boustifaille* la graille*
to eat	bouffer* grailler*
to be hungry	avoir la fringale* avoir un creux
to be dying of hunger	crever de faim
it gives one an appetite	ça creuse
can we start?	alors, on attaque?

a snack	un casse-croûte ("la croûte" here is the end of the long French bread "la baguette"; you would be breaking off a piece of the "baguette" to have a snack with cheese, chocolate, pâté, etc.)
to have a bite	casser la croûte
to have a hearty appetite	avoir un bon coup de fourchette (literally, to have a good way with the fork)
to stuff one's face	s'empiffrer* s'en mettre plein la lampe se taper la cloche
to shovel it in	bouffer à la pelle*
to polish off	se farcir* se payer*
a gourmet	une fine-gueule
a glutton	un goinfre
a feast	un gueuleton*
to be full	caler
to have enough to feed an army	en avoir assez pour un régiment
watery soup	la lavasse* (literally, dishwater)

potatoes	les patates (f.)
beans	les fayots (m.)
cheese	le frometon le frome
meat	la bidoche
tough meat	la barbaque* la carne*
it's as tough as shoe leather	c'est de la semelle (la semelle = the sole of a shoe)
to hack away at the roast	charcuter le rôti
salami	le sauciflard
the leftovers	les rogatons
pigswill, bilge	la ragougnasse*
a fridge	un frigo
to do the cooking	faire la tambouille* faire la popote
awful cooking	la tambouille*
to burn	cramer*
smells of burned fat	les odeurs (f.) de graillon*
a café	un bistro(t)
a restaurant	un resto

a seedy-looking little eating place	un boui-boui*
a cook	un cuistot*
the bill, the <u>damage</u>	la douleureuse (literally, the painful one)
to <u>fleece the customer</u>	écorcher le client (écorcher = to skin)
this place is a rip off	c'est le coup de fusil ici

DRINK

wine	le pinard
red wine	le rouquin (rouquin,e = red-haired)
ordinary red wine	le gros rouge qui tache et qui pousse au crime (literally, the thick red wine that stains and incites to crime) le gros rouge (short for the above)
cheap wine	la piquette*
a little glass of wine	un petit canon
a liter bottle	un litron
the empties	les cadavres (m.)
weak, low-quality alcohol	la bibine*

70

rot-gut	le tord-boyaux*
any weak beverage (coffee, etc.)	du pipi* d'âne (literally, donkey's piss) du pipi* de chat (literally, cat's piss)
a drop	une larme (literally, a tear)
galore	à gogo (as in "il y avait du whiskey à gogo" = there was whiskey galore)
a cocktail	un apéro (short for "un apéritif")
to have a drink	boire un coup prendre un pot
to celebrate an event with a drink	arroser un évènement
this calls for a celebration!	ça s'arrose!
cheers!	tchin tchin!
to be partial to red wine	marcher au rouge carburer au rouge
to dilute one's wine with water	baptiser son vin
to be tipsy	avoir un coup dans l'aile être pompette
to have had one too many	avoir un verre dans le nez

to get smashed	se saouler la gueule**
	se cuiter*
	se payer une bonne cuite*
plastered, drunk	paf*
	rond,e
	rond,e comme une bille
	bourré,e*
	blindé,e*
	schlass*
to be a boozer	picoler*
a lush	une éponge* (literally, a sponge)
a boozer	un picoleur*
	un soiffard*
	un boit-sans-soif*
a drunkard	un soulard*
	un soulot*
	un poivrot*

VOUS ÊTES UN CLODO ET UN POIVROT!

| to have a hangover | avoir la gueule de bois*
(literally, to have a
wooden mouth) |
| to sleep one's drink off | cuver son vin |

HOW ABOUT THESE SENTENCES?

1. Qu'est-ce qu'on bouffe? Je crève de faim!

2. Les journalistes, ça picole drôlement.

3. Les anglais sont bien sympas mais leur tambouille est dégueulasse.

4. Venez prendre un pot dimanche.

5. Oh merde, j'ai cramé la bidoche.

6. Les goinfres se sont farcis tout le rôti.

7. On a fait la nouba chez les Dupont: y'avait du champagne à gogo, tout le monde était paf, ça dégueulait partout.

1. What are we eating? I'm dying of hunger!

2. Journalists are real boozers.

3. The English are awfully nice but their cooking is disgusting.

4. Come and have a drink on Sunday.

5. Oh, hell, I burned the meat.

6. The gluttons polished off all the roast.

7. We whooped it up at the Duponts: there was champagne galore, everyone was drunk, people were puking everywhere.

VI
HASSLING

With your average Frenchman bristling with impatience toward all other mortals, it is inevitable that there should be a number of words describing forms of aggression or the threat and result of its use.

chicken	dégonflé,e
to chicken out	se dégonfler (literally, to lose all one's air)
cowardly, lily-livered	froussard,e trouillard,e
fear	la frousse la pétoche la trouille
to be afraid	avoir la frousse avoir la pétoche

	avoir la trouille
	avoir les jetons (pronounce this "chton")
to squabble	se chamailler
to get pissed off	se foutre** en rogne se foutre** en boule
to be hopping mad	être furax* être furibard,e* être furibond,e*
to tell someone off	attraper quelqu'un passer un savon à quelqu'un secouer les puces à quelqu'un (literally, to shake someone's fleas) enguirlander* engueuler**
to get a lecture	se faire attraper se faire passer un savon se faire secouer les puces se faire enguirlander* se faire engueuler** se faire sonner les cloches
a fight	une prise de bec*
a racket, an uproar	un chahut
to bug the teacher	chahuter le prof
a fight between women, a cat fight	un crêpage de chignon (le chignon = bun, the hairstyle; crêper = to

	tease, to crimp hair, so you get the image of women tearing at each other's hair in that nasty female way of fighting)
to kick up a stink, to make a racket	faire du boucan faire du raffut faire du barouf
to yell	gueuler**
there is going to be trouble	ça va barder ça va chauffer il va y avoir du grabuge il va y avoir de la casse (violent trouble)
things are heating up	ça barde ça sent le roussi (roussi = burned, scorched)
to give someone a rough time	faire passer un mauvais quart d'heure à quelqu'un
to be on the verge of doing something nasty	aller faire un malheur (as in "je vais faire un malheur" = I'm about to do something horrible)
to be at one another's throats	se bouffer le nez*
to slap	allonger une baffe flanquer une baffe ficher* une baffe foutre** une baffe

a blow, a punch	une beigne
	une taloche
	un marron
	une châtaigne
	une pêche
a black eye	un oeil au beurre noir
a knock, a blow	un gnon
to scuffle, to brawl	se bagarrer
a scuffle, a brawl	une bagarre

77

a spanking	une fessée
to fly at	voler dans les plumes de*
to have a fistfight	se tabasser se taper dessus
to punch someone in the face	envoyer le poing à la figure de quelqu'un
to smash someone's face in	casser la figure à quelqu'un* casser la gueule à quelqu'un** abîmer le portrait de quelqu'un* faire une grosse tête à quelqu'un
to give someone a beating	flanquer une trempe/raclée à quelqu'un ficher* une trempe/raclée à quelqu'un foutre** une trempe/raclée à quelqu'un
to kick ass	botter les fesses*
to tear one another's guts out	s'étriper*
to send someone flying	envoyer quelqu'un valser (literally, to send someone waltzing)
to total	amocher bousiller
to faint	tomber dans les pommes

78

to be unconscious	être dans le cirage (le cirage = the boot polish)
to waste, to kill	zigouiller
to eliminate (to get rid of or to kill)	liquider
to bump off	buter descendre
to shoot someone	flinguer quelqu'un foutre** une balle dans la peau* de quelqu'un
a gun	un flingue, un flingot
a police van, paddy wagon	un panier à salade
prison	la taule, la tôle

QUIZ TIME

1. Les gosses ont besoin qu'on leur foute des baffes de temps en temps.

2. Espèce de salaud, je vais te casser la gueule.

3. Le mec avait tellement la frousse qu'il est tombé dans les pommes.

4. Les gangsters ont été foutus en taule après avoir descendu leurs rivaux.

5. Je vais me faire secouer les puces parce que j'ai foutu un oeil au beurre noir à mon frangin.

1. Kids need to be slapped from time to time.

2. You bastard, I'll smash your face in.

3. The guy was so scared he fainted.

4. The gangsters were thrown into prison after having bumped off their rivals.

5. I'm going to get a lecture because I gave my brother a black eye.

VII
MONEY MATTERS

money	le fric
	le pognon
	le pèze
	la galette
	la braise
	l'oseille (f.)
	les ronds (m.)
	le flouse
loose change	la ferraille (literally, scrap iron)
francs	les balles (f.) (as in "ça coûte quinze balles" = it costs fifteen francs)
10,000 francs	une brique
to be broke	être fauché,e
	être à sec

not to have a cent	ne pas avoir un radis (le radis = radish)
	ne pas avoir un rond
filthy rich	rupin,e*
a spoiled daddy's boy	un fils à papa
to be loaded	être plein,e aux as
mean	radin,e
a skin-flint	un grippe-sous
to fork out	casquer
to blow	claquer
to be had	se faire avoir
to con, to rip off	rouler
	couillonner**
it's a fake, it's imitation	c'est du toc
junk, rubbish	de la camelote
expensive	chéro
free	à l'oeil
profit	le bénef (short for "le bénéfice" = the gain, profit)

PRACTICE MAKES PERFECT

1. Dis, t'as du fric à me passer? Je suis fauché et je dois 100 basses à mon copain.

2. Ce petit fils à papa a claqué un pognon fou sur de la camelote.

3. J'ai eu ces billets à l'oeil.

4. Ce salaud t'a roulé; t'as casqué une fortune pour du toc.

1. Hey, have you got any money to lend me? I'm broke and I owe my friend 100 francs.

2. That little daddy's boy blew an awful lot of money on junk.

3. I got these tickets free.

4. That bastard ripped you off; you forked out a fortune on fake junk.

VIII
WORK AND SOCIAL STATUS

WORK AND JOBS

work, the job	le boulot
the workplace	la boîte
to work	bosser boulonner
to work hard	bûcher
hard-working	bûcheur, euse
laziness	la cosse la flemme
lazy	flemmard, e
to be lazy	avoir un poil dans la main

a failure	un raté, une ratée
to exploit	faire suer le burnous* (suer = to perspire, le burnous = an Arabian robe-like garment; from the "good old days" of the Empire when one made Arabs work like slaves)
to fire, to <u>kick out</u>, to give the boot	vider (literally, empty out) foutre** à la porte
to have friends in the right places	avoir du piston
string pulling	le piston
to pull strings on behalf of someone	pistonner quelqu'un
to <u>grease someone's palm</u>	graisser la patte à quelqu'un*
a bigwig	une grosse légume un gros bonnet une huile
a <u>cop</u>, a policeman	un flic un poulet
the <u>fuzz</u>, the police	la flicaille*
down with the pigs!	mort aux vaches!**
a motorcycle cop	une vache à roulettes**

a member of the security/ espionage services	un barbouze
a bodyguard	un gorille
a doctor	un toubib
a teacher	un prof
a chef	un cuistot*

QUAND J'SUIS GRAND, J'VAIS ÊTRE TOUBIB ET AVOIR PLEIN DE FRIC !

a funeral parlor employee	un croque-mort* (croquer = to bite into, to munch)
a priest in his cassock	un corbeau* (literally, a crow)
a politician	un politicard*
a female rest room attendant	une dame-pipi*
a cobbler	un bouif*
a painter (the artistic sort)	un barbouilleur* (barbouiller = to smear, to scrawl)
third-rate paintings	les croûtes* (f.)
a third-rate book, film or other work of art	un navet
a paper-pusher (usually a bureaucrat)	un rond-de-cuir*
a soldier	un troufion*

SOCIAL STATUS AND POLITICAL AFFILIATION

a hick, a bumpkin	un plouc, une ploucquesse* un pécore* un péquenaud* un pedzouille*

a peasant	un cul-terreux** (literally, one whose ass is covered in earth)
	un bouseux** (from "la bouse de vache" = cow dung)
the country (as opposed to the city)	la cambrousse*
the sticks	la brousse
a village	un patelin*
a real hole	un trou*
	un bled*
to live in the boondocks	habiter au feu de dieu
	habiter à perpète ("perpète" is short for "la perpétuité," conveying the notion of great distance)
a tramp	un clodo*
the lower classes, the masses	le populo*
a prole (proletarian)	un prolo*
an aristocrat	un aristo*
the upper crust	le gratin
a Parisian	un parigot, une parigote* (Parisians hold a high rank in the social

	hierarchy; provincials are considered virtually subhuman)
a reactionary	un réac*
a fascist	un facho*
a commie	un coco*
an anarchist	un anar*
a demonstration	une manif (short for "la manifestation" = the demonstration)

TEST YOUR KNOWLEDGE

1. Les seules gonzesses qui sont promues dans cette sale boîte sont les pouffiasses qui se laissent baiser par le patron ou les salopes qui ont du piston.

2. Les toubibs donnent beaucoup de boulot aux croque-morts.

3. Un plouc, ça se voit à dix mètres.

4. La punition la plus sévère pour les aristos, à l'époque des rois, c'était l'exil à la cambrousse.

5. Comment, ma fille épouser un cul-terreux et aller habiter à perpète dans un bled perdu? Pas question.

6. A la manif, les fachos ont foutu une trempe aux cocos.

1. The only women who get promoted in this damn company are the sluts who let the boss screw them or the bitches who have friends in the right places.

2. Quacks give a lot of work to undertakers.

3. You can tell a hick ten meters away.

4. In the days of the kings the most severe punishment for the aristocrats was exile to the country.

5. What, my daughter marry a peasant and live in the boondocks, in some godforsaken hole? Certainly not.

6. At the demonstration the fascists beat up the commies.

IX
INDULGING IN RACISM, XENOPHOBIA AND DISRESPECT FOR ONE'S ELDERS

The innate French feeling of superiority extends of course to the Americans, but this is a love-hate, smugness-envy relationship. Slang words for Americans are pretty tame—no stronger or more offending than "yank." Other nations don't get off so lightly.

a limey, a Brit	un bifteck* (= a steak)
	un rosbif* (= a roast-beef)
a kraut	un boche**
	un chleuh**
	un fritz**
	un frisé**
	un fridolin**
a dago	un rastaquouère** (this has generally meant a greasy foreigner but usually equals dago)

91

a wop	un rital**
	un macaroni**
a Russian	un ruski*
	un ruskof*
a chink	un chinetoque**
an Arab	un bougnoule**
	un bicot**
a North African Arab (the French bugbear)	un raton** (gives rise to "la ratonnade" = mob Arab-bashing)
	un melon**
	un crouille**
	un noraf
Jewish	baptisé au sécateur* (literally, baptized with pruning shears)
an old granddad	un vieux pépé*
an old granny	une vieille mémé*
an old biddy	une vieille toupie*
an old fogey	un vieux schnoque*
	un vieux bonze*
an old hag, a crone	une vieille bique* (la bique = the nanny-goat)
	une vieille rombière*
	une vieille taupe*

to speak pidgin French

parler petit nègre
parler le français comme
une vache espagnole

HERE IS ANOTHER EXERCISE FOR YOU

1. Les boches bossent dur, mais les ritals sont flemmards.

2. Les amerloques sont de grands enfants.

3. C'est un quartier de ratons.

4. Allez, bouge ton cul, vieille bique.

5. Moi, j'peux pas sentir les vieux schnoques.

1. Krauts work hard, but wops are lazy.

2. Americans are big kids.

3. It's an Arab neighborhood.

4. Come on, move your ass, old hag.

5. I can't stand old fogeys.

X
TO EXIT RAPIDLY

to <u>shove off</u>, to <u>get the hell out</u>	filer se barrer se tailler se tirer déguerpir se débiner ficher*/foutre** le camp
to hurry up	se magner se dégrouiller se grouiller
get lost! get out!	allez, oust! dégagez! débarrassez le plancher!
to kick out	vider balancer foutre** à la porte

APPLY YOUR KNOWLEDGE

1. Hé, les mômes, foutez-moi le camp d'ici! Alalez, magnez-vous ou j'appelle les flics.

2. Filons avant que la maternelle n'arrive.

1. Hey, kids, clear out! Come on, hurry up or I'll call the cops.

2. Let's get the hell out of here before the old lady comes.

XI
POSITIVE THINKING

Although the Frenchman's bent is for the scathing remark, he is able to whip up enthusiasm.

great, fantastic (used as an adjective or as an exclamation)

formidable, formide
terrible
sensas (short for "sensationel")
super
génial,e
chouette (when used as an adjective, it is placed before the noun, not after as others are)
impeccable
au poil (don't confuse with "a poil" which, as you no doubt remember, means "naked")
extra

great, fantastic (used only as an adjective)	bath
	chié,e**
	chiadé,e**
	du tonnerre

| to have great success | avoir un succès boeuf |

| to have great effect | avoir un effet boeuf |

TRY YOUR HAND AT THESE SENTENCES

1. Chouette, les vacances sont arrivées!
2. Elle est super, ta bagnole!
3. J'ai lu un bouquin sensas.
4. Elle est chouette, ta frangine!
5. Cette pièce a eu un succès boeuf.

1. Great, the holidays are here!
2. Your car is fantastic!
3. I read a fabulous book.
4. Your sister is great!
5. This play had tremendous success.

XII
FOREIGN INVASIONS OF THE LANGUAGE

READ THE FOLLOWING

1. C'est un appartement de grand standing, avec parking.

2. Quel était le score au match?

3. Les gangsters ont effectué un raid pendant le meeting. Le holdup leur a rapporté 10,000 dollars.

4. J'ai acheté ce gadget au stand du fond.

5. Au club, certains étaient en smoking, d'autres en jeans et pull.

6. J'ai acheté un sandwich au self-service.

7. Le cameraman a pris des films pendant l'interview.

8. Le leader du parti souffre de stress.

9. On a fait du stop.

Recognize some of the words? "Franglais," that insidious creeping of English words into the French language, is a source of worry to the French authorities but is proving hard to contain. All the words above are used in conversation and in the media; they aren't considered colloquial. Therefore, the above sentences are not an attempt at being funny, they are examples of contemporary French! In passing from English to French, however, some words have undergone a little transformation, so here are the translations:

1. It's a luxury apartment with parking facilities.

2. What was the score at the game?

3. The gangsters carried out a raid during the meeting. The holdup netted them 10,000 dollars.

4. I bought this gadget at the stand at the back.

5. At the club some were wearing dinner jackets, others jeans and sweaters.

6. I bought a sandwich at the self-service restaurant.

7. The cameraman filmed during the interview.

8. The party's leader is suffering from stress.

9. We hitchhiked.

From the former North African colonies come some Arab words which are firmly implanted in French colloquial vocabulary:

no; no way; nothing	oualou
a hole (the boondocks type, remember?)	un bled*
the same	kif-kif

a little (quantity)	un chouïa
luck	la baraka
not much, nothing much	pas bézef
the boss	le caïd
money	le flouse

IMPROVE YOUR COLLOQUIAL USAGE
FROM THE FOLLOWING

1. "Vous prenez du cafe?" "Un chouïa."

2. Y'a pas bézef à faire dans ce bled.

3. "Tu veux le rouge ou le bleu?" "Oh, n'importe, c'est kif-kif."

4. Le caïd a de la baraka.

1. "Will you have some coffee?" "A little."

2. There's not much to do in this hole.

3. "Do you want the red one or the blue one?" "Oh, it doesn't matter, it's the same."

4. The boss has luck on his side.

XIII
YOUR FINAL EXAM

Identify the literary tales or historical figures. Answers, but not translations, are provided on the following page.

1. Ce mec devait être vachement frustré parce que c'était un nabot. Sa bergère, qui était un peu bougnoule sur les bords, voulait toujours qu'il la baise, mais il répondait "Pas ce soir, Josephine" parce qu'il était toujours en train de se bagarrer (avec les boches, les ruskis, etc.). Elle l'a cocufié. Les anglais lui ont foutu une vraie trempe, l'ont exilé dans un bled infâme et l'ont probablement empoisonné avec leur tambouille infecte.

2. Y'a deux familles d'aristos ritals qui sont en rogne et puis le fiston de l'une a le béguin pour la fille de l'autre. Il se la farcit, mais ils ont la frousse de dire à leurs vieux qu'ils sont enamourachés, alors ils se zigouillent. A la fin, toute la bande de cons chiale et devient copains.

3. Un piaf avait chipé un frome et allait juste le bouffer quand un renard fait un peu de lèche-cul pour lui faire ouvrir la

gueule. Le frome tombe, le renard le pique et déguerpit avec.

4. C'etait un roi, un gros lard mais pas con. Il est devenu parpaillot pour balancer sa bobonne, dont il avait ras le bol. D'autres bobonnes, quand elles l'emmerdaient, il les a faites zigouiller.

ANSWERS

1. Napoleon
2. Romeo and Juliet
3. Aesop's fable of the fox and the crow
4. Henry VIII

ASSESSMENT

0 correct = Connard!
1 correct = Dégueulasse!
2 correct = Flemmard!
3 correct = Sympa!
4 correct = Sensas!